Sound

C O N C E P T   S C I E N C E

Written by Colin Walker

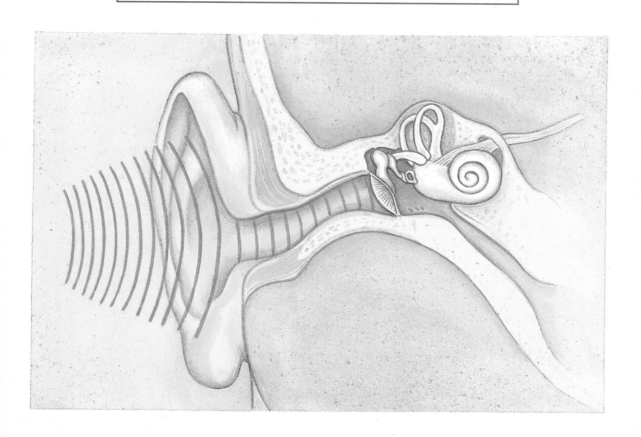

From the time we wake up until the time we go to bed, we hear many different sounds.

In the morning, we may wake up to the sounds of the alarm clock, the radio, or birds singing.

On the way to school,
we hear different sounds
like the wind blowing,
the bus coming, or the
sound of the school bell.

3

Sounds are made when
something vibrates.

A guitar string vibrates and
the sound travels to our ears.
The voice box in our throat
vibrates when we talk.

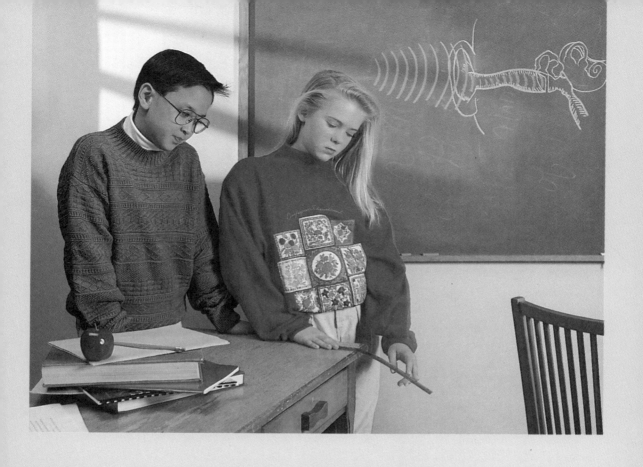

When a drum is beaten, it vibrates.
A tuning fork vibrates when we hit it.

When a ruler is plucked, we can
see it vibrating.

Sound travels through the air, and sound travels through water too.

When we are swimming under water, we can hear other people splashing and talking.

7

Fish have special organs
along the sides of their body.
They can feel sound vibrations
as they swim.

Whales and dolphins use sound
to communicate with each other
through water.

Sound travels through solid things, too,
like the earth. North American Indians
used to listen to the ground for the
sound of horses' hooves.

Messages can be tapped along
pipes, wires, or through walls.

With a string telephone you can send
and receive messages.

Sound vibrations are used to make
a pattern on a record, compact disc,
or video tape. When we play these,
we can hear the sound again.

The sounds you hear from the speakers may be played loudly or softly. The speakers vibrate to make the sounds.

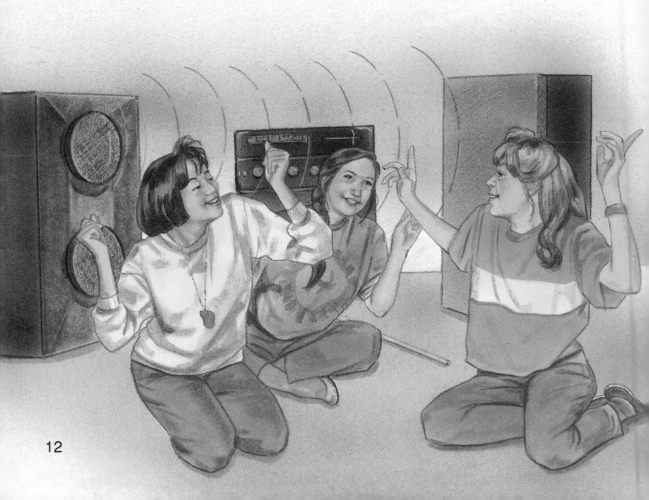

Some animals, like the cat and the horse, have ears that can hear sounds very well.

Their ears are big and funnel-shaped to catch the sounds easily. They can turn their ears toward the sounds too.

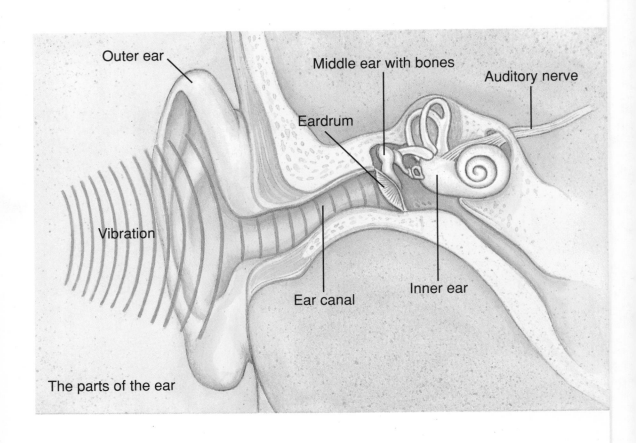

Outer ear

Middle ear with bones

Auditory nerve

Eardrum

Vibration

Ear canal

Inner ear

The parts of the ear

Our ears feel the sound vibrations.

We hear sounds that travel through
solids, through liquids, and through
the air.

14

QUIZ

When something vibrates, we hear _____ .

Sound travels through _____ , _____ , and _____ .

Name two things on which we can record sound vibrations.

How do fish hear sounds through the water?

How can we hear sounds through water?

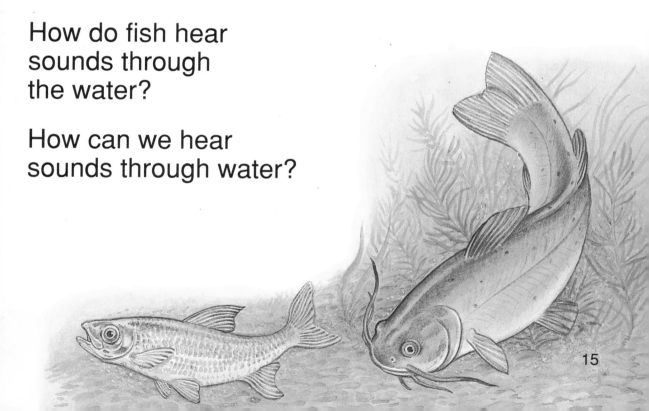

15

Try these activities:

1. Make a list of all the sounds you hear at home for one hour. Share your list with a small group of students. Together, sort the sounds into categories such as noisy, musical, loud, or soft.

2. Knock on a table with your fist. Then knock on the same table, but this time place something soft like a sweater or a pillow between your hand and the table. Why do the knocks sound different? What does the soft object do to the sound? Work with a friend to make a list of things in your classroom that help absorb sounds.